The ABC's of Honey Bees

Roda Shope

The ABC's of Honey Bees
© Roda Shope 2020

www.indigoacresapiary.com

All rights reserved. No portion of this book may be reproduced,
stored in a retrieval system, or transmitted in any form or by any means,
mechanical, electronic, photocopying, recording, or otherwise,
without written permission.

Published in the United Kingdom by
Northern Bee Books,
Scout Bottom Farm,
Mytholmroyd,
West Yorkshire HX7 5JS
Tel: 01422 882751
Fax: 01422 886157
www.northernbeebooks.co.uk

ISBN 978-1-912271-78-8

Photography by Roda Shope
Design and artwork, DM Design and Print

The ABC's of Honey Bees

Roda Shope

To my favorite queen bee
who told me to just put the hive in the cart...

About the Author

Roda has always had a passion for nature and the arts. With her camera and sketch pad in hand, she spent her childhood exploring the woods, chasing bees, and gardening with her dad. As a young adult, she continued to celebrate nature through storytelling, art, and photography and shared these passions throughout her 20+ year career as an elementary educator. In 2014, Roda's lifelong beekeeping dream became a reality, and Indigo Acres Apiary was born. Roda's love for education continues as she shares knowledge with others about the importance of pollinators and the plants that sustain them. It is her hope that *The ABC's of Honey Bees* will inspire others to support, protect, and celebrate these magical creatures. Roda lives with her family in Rockford, Michigan.

Acknowledgments

Thank you to my bee-utiful children, Cam, Ben, and Ella, for putting up with my constant bee babble. I am grateful for their love and support even if they always take my commas away. Thank you to my Dad, for his gardening passion and for instilling in me the meaning of true work ethic. Many thanks to my amazing bee ladies: Erin, Kelly, Mindy, and Wendy for trusting me with their bee journeys. I am forever thankful for my little bro, Jay, not only for his wisdom, but for his patience with the amount of words I need to say in a single conversation. Thank you to Mandy from bellabeek.com for her friendship and ability to create the most beautiful bee veils. I am grateful for my dear friend Kathleen, for being a true inspiration and role model throughout my life. Many thanks to Jeremy at NBB for giving me the opportunity to share my passion and to David for his guidance throughout the publishing process.

An extra special thanks to Paul, a true creative Jedi, for his multitude of talents and uncanny attention to detail.

Most importantly, I am forever thankful for Sandy, for her unconditional love and never-ending support regardless of what crazy ideas I might conjure up next.

Apiary

An **apiary** is an outside location where **colonies** of honey bees are kept in bee **hives**. Apiaries come in many sizes and can be found in both urban and rural settings.

Brood

The term **brood** refers to all of the immature stages of the honey bee: eggs, larvae, and pupae.

Cell

Comb (built from **beeswax**) is made up of individual, hexagonal openings called **cells.**
Honey bees use these cells to raise their young and store resources such as pollen and honey.

Drone

A male honey bee is known as a **drone**. His role in the colony is to mate with the queen. This stocky fellow has extremely large eyes and is unable to defend the hive, for he has no stinger. In the fall, the female worker bees escort the drones out of the hive and prevent them from re-entering. Because drones are unable to forage for resources, they quickly perish in the outdoor elements. Once spring arrives, the drone population will reestablish within the colony.

Eggs

The **egg** is the first stage of the honey bee's life cycle. Each tiny, white egg is laid by the queen in the middle of a cell. The egg is approximately 1.5 mm in length. This is equivalent to half the size of a single grain of rice.

Forage

Honey bees **forage**, or search, for both pollen and nectar from flowers.

Pollen is a protein food source for the bees. This powdery substance is collected from flowers by the forager bees, brought back to the hive, and stored in cells.

Nectar is the sweet liquid secreted by plants in bloom. The bees gather nectar and convert it into honey.

Garden

A wonderful way to attract **pollinators** is by planting a pollinator-friendly backyard garden. By providing blooms throughout the seasons, local bees, hummingbirds, and butterflies will flourish year-round.

Hive

A constructed or natural structure used by a **colony** of honey bees as their home.

Italian Honey Bee

Proboscis: The honey bee's proboscis is a straw-like tongue. It is structured much like a straw within a straw. The outer straw is used for sucking water and honey. The inner straw is used for collecting nectar from flowers.

Eyes: A honey bee has five eyes. The two large **compound eyes** are used for general distance. The three small simple eyes, called **ocelli**, are used in poor lighting conditions inside the hive. In this photo, you can see one of the small ocelli on top of this bee's head.

Antennae: Did you know that a honey bee does not have a nose but has an incredible sense of smell? Using their antennae, these amazing creatures are able to locate hundreds of nectar and pollen-rich floral varieties, even while in flight.

Wings: The honey bee's wings stroke about 200 beats per second, thus making that well-known "buzz".

Mandibles: The honey bee's mandibles (jaws) act as a personal hive tool. These mandibles are useful for any task that requires carrying, cutting, or pinching. The mandible's edges are sharp, providing enough force to kill a honey bee's enemy.

Jobs

Every member of a honey bee colony has a purpose. While the queen is busy laying as many as 1,500 eggs per day, the worker bees are hard at work nurturing and feeding the huge appetites of the young **larvae**.

Kindness

When a bee is visiting a flower,
remember she is just doing her job.
By collecting food for her **colony**,
she is also giving us the gift of **pollination**!

Larva

The second stage of a honey bee's life cycle is the larval stage. Approximately three days after the queen bee lays an egg, it hatches into a tiny **larva**. This larva will grow at an amazing rate. In only five days, a female larva will grow more than 1,500 times her original size!

Mating Flight

After a new queen bee emerges from her queen cell,
she will prepare for her mating flight.
The young queen will mate with
multiple drones 200 to 300 feet in the air.

Nectar Flow

Nectar Flow is the time of year when major nectar producing plants are in bloom. Bees gather nectar and convert it to honey.

Orientation Flight

Honey bees partake in multiple flights directly in front of their hive. These flights are known as **"orientation flights"**. These short flights allow the bees to become familiar with their surroundings. After foraging for resources (such a pollen and nectar) miles away from home, it is essential that bees know where their hive is located.

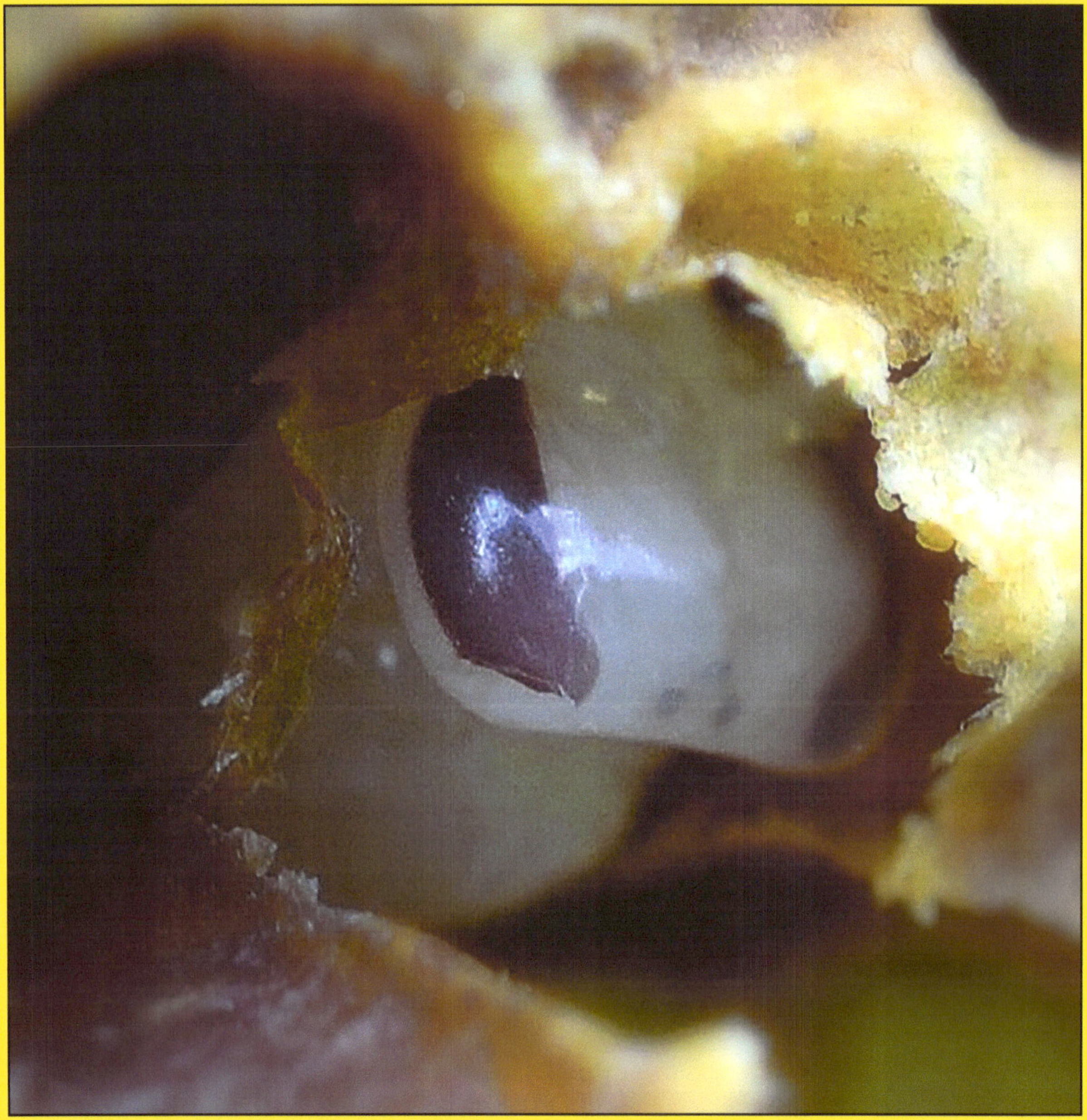

Pupa

The third stage of the honey bee's life cycle is the pupal stage. Once the worker bees seal a **larva** inside a cell using beeswax, the larva will spin a cocoon around its entire body. From this point on, the larva is referred to as a "**pupa**". After being sealed inside her cell for 12 days, the new female worker bee will chew her way out of the cell and begin her role in the colony.

Queen

Although the queen bee is the largest bee in the colony, she is extremely gentle. Unlike worker bees, queen bees can sting numerous times. However, they only use their stingers to defend themselves from other queens.
The queen has two main roles in the colony. Her first role is to sustain the population of the colony by laying lots and lots of eggs. Her second role is to produce chemical scents, called **pheromones,** to communicate order and to set the tone within the hive.

Royal Jelly

This highly nutritious substance is secreted from the glands of young worker bees. **Royal jelly** is used to feed both young larvae and queen bee larvae.

Supersedure

When a **colony** decides to replace its current queen, due to age or illness, they will create numerous **supersedure cells**. The first queen to emerge from her cell will eliminate her competition, by stinging through the remaining queen cells. The worker bees will then remove the cells and repurpose the wax.

Teamwork

Festooning is when a group of female worker bees connect together leg-by-leg between frames. These little ladies sure take the idea of teamwork to the next level!

Useful

About 1/3 of the world's food supply depends on
pollinating insects like honey bees.
Let's make sure we take extra special care of these
little friends that work so hard pollinating
the food we eat!

Venom

When a honey bee stings in self-defense, **venom** (a poisonous fluid) is released into the skin. Removing the stinger quickly and carefully will reduce the uncomfortable reaction caused by the honey bee venom.

Worker Bee

A female worker bee's job is never done. She spends the early part of her life tending to the young **larvae**, as a nurse bee. She spends the last half of her life outside of the hive foraging for pollen and nectar. During her lifetime she will produce just 1/12th of a teaspoon of honey!

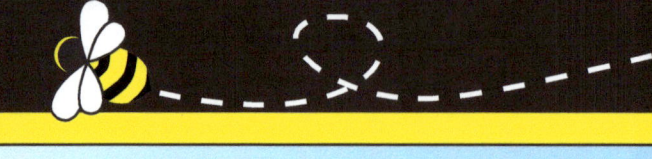

eXoskeleton

Unlike a human, a honey bee's skeleton is on the outside of their body rather than the inside. The **exoskeleton** not only supports the honey bee's body, but it protects their internal organs like a suit of armor.

Young

This golden beauty just emerged from her cell. As time passes, her color will darken, and her fuzziness will disappear. Although she is often referred to as a "baby" bee due to her fuzzy appearance, this is not the case; she is a full-grown adult bee, ready to take on her role in the colony.

Zoom

A honey bee beats her wings approximately 12,000 times per minute! The honey bee is always hard at work pollinating much of the food we eat daily. The next time you spot a bee in your backyard, thank her for her hard work!

Dear Reader,

As a beekeeper and avid gardener, it is my mission to spread awareness about the significance of honey bees and other pollinators. Did you know that these amazing creatures pollinate 1/3 of the food we eat? That's one in every three bites! Just think of the powerful impact we would have if each of us took one tiny step toward pollinator protection…

How YOU Can Help Your Local Pollinators!

 Plant pollinator friendly plants, shrubs, and trees. Soon your backyard will be bursting with hummingbirds, bees, and butterflies. Select flowers that will provide blooms throughout the changing seasons. Remember, even if you have a small space, potted plants work well too.

 Please allow the dandelions to flourish! The dandelion is the perfect flower—no purchase required. All you have to do is let this wildflower grow. Dandelions are one of the first spring food sources for the bees. Please, let them live!

 Provide a shallow water source. The saucers used under garden pots work well for this. Submerge rocks half-way underwater to act as a landing pad. Your backyard water source will keep your local pollinators happy and hydrated.

Avoid the use of pesticides. These harmful chemicals kill our beneficial insect population.

 Support your local, pollinator friendly farmers and beekeepers by purchasing organic produce and raw honey.

 Leave dead stumps and tree trunks for wood-nesting insects.

 Allow an area of your backyard to grow WILD! This natural space will provide a safe haven for many pollinators.

 BEE an advocate! Use your voice to help protect not only our honey bees, but all of our beneficial pollinators.

Together we WILL make a difference!

Let's BEE Inspired!

Roda

Glossary

Antennae - The sensory organ honey bees use to detect odor.

Apiary - An outside location where colonies of honey bees are kept in bee hives.

Beeswax - A substance secreted by honey bees used to construct honey comb.

Brood - The immature stages of the honey bee: eggs, larvae, and pupae.

Cell - An individual, hexagonal opening made from beeswax.

Colony - A family of honey bees.

Comb - A group of wax cells connected together.

Compound Eyes - The two large eyes of the honey bee used for general distance.

Drone - A male honey bee.

Egg - The first stage of the honey bee's life cycle.

Exoskeleton - A hard covering on the outside of the body that supports and protects the honey bee.

Festooning - A group of female worker bees connecting together leg-by-leg between frames.

Forage - To search for resources from the environment.

Garden - An area of land where plants are grown.

Hive - A constructed or natural structure used by a colony of honey bees as their home.

Larva - (*plural* larvae) An immature, grub-like insect with a huge appetite.

Mandibles - The jaws of the honey bee.

Mating Flight - The act in which the queen bee leaves the hive to mate with numerous drones (male honey bees).

Nectar - The sweet liquid secreted by plants in bloom.

Nectar Flow - The time of year when major nectar producing plants are in bloom.

Ocelli - The three small simple eyes of the honey bee used in poor lighting conditions inside the hive.

Orientation Flight - A short flight that allows the bees to become familiar with their surroundings.

Pheromones - The chemicals released by the queen bee to communicate order within the hive.

Pollen - A powdery substance collected from flowers by forager bees.

Pollination - The transfer of pollen from one plant to another allowing plants to reproduce.

Pollinator - An animal that transfers pollen from one plant to another.

Proboscis - The straw-like tongue of the honey bee.

Pupa - (*plural* pupae) An inactive insect sealed inside a cocoon.

Queen Bee - A large, fully developed female bee with the main purpose of laying eggs.

Royal Jelly - A highly nutritious substance that is secreted from the glands of young worker bees.

Supersedure - The process of replacing an old queen bee with a new one.

Venom - A poisonous fluid that is released from the stinger of a honey bee.

Worker Bees -Female bees that make up the majority of the colony.

www.ingramcontent.com/pod-product-compliance
Lightning Source LLC
Chambersburg PA
CBHW060820090426

42738CB00002B/51